"THE SWIMMING POOL IS FANTASTIC, BUT IS THERE ENOUGH CLOSET SPACE?"

"IS THERE SHOPPING NEARBY? WHAT ABOUT THE NEIGHBORHOOD SCHOOLS?"

"IS THIS HOUSE WORTH WHAT THEY'RE ASKING FOR IT?"

From first look to closing, this concise, easy-to-use guide is the home buyer's best friend. *It's your move—so make it as rewarding and trouble-free as possible!*

ABOUT THE AUTHOR

EDWIN L. HOSEUS, MREC, is a licensed broker/realtor in Ohio and Kentucky with over 40 years of experience in the field. He has earned the title of Master Real Estate Consultant from the National Institute for Real Estate Consultants. He is married and lives in Cincinnati, Ohio.

The Home Buyer's Checklists

EDWIN L. HOSEUS

AVON BOOKS ◢ NEW YORK

This publication is designed to provide accurate and authoritative information in regard to the subject matter covered. It cannot, necessarily, be
completely comprehensive. Real estate conditions, laws and tax implica-
tions vary by locality. This book is sold with the understanding that the
publisher and author are not engaged in rendering legal, accounting or
other professional service. If legal advice or other expert assistance is
required, the services of a competent professional should be sought.

AVON BOOKS
A division of
The Hearst Corporation
105 Madison Avenue
New York, New York 10016

Copyright © 1986, 1991 by Edwin L. Hoseus
Published by arrangement with the author
Library of Congress Catalog Card Number: 90-93557
ISBN: 0-380-76122-X

First Avon Books Printing: March 1991

AVON TRADEMARK REG. U.S. PAT. OFF. AND IN OTHER COUNTRIES, MARCA
REGISTRADA, HECHO EN U.S.A.

Printed in the U.S.A.

RA 10 9 8 7 6 5 4 3 2 1

For the Buyer—A Friend in Need

———————

The author gives recognition to the research facilities of the Department of Housing and Urban Development (HUD), the Kentucky Real Estate Center and the Ohio Association of Realtors.

___ ALERT ___

Follow these *recommendations* for the most *rewarding use* of this book.

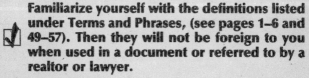

Familiarize yourself with the definitions listed under Terms and Phrases, (see pages 1–6 and 49–57). Then they will not be foreign to you when used in a document or referred to by a realtor or lawyer.

Take these checklists with you when looking for a home.

Check either the ALERT or OK box for each item.

Obtain a satisfactory answer for any ALERT box that you have checked.

Use the checklists in the suggested sequence. These were designed to help you buy your home in an informed and logical manner.

CONTENTS

*Use these chapters *in addition* to those that precede them when buying a condominium.

1
REAL ESTATE TERMS AND PHRASES

It is suggested that you become familiar with these terms and phrases that are found in real estate documents and referred to by realtors and lawyers:

Absolute Fee Simple Title
The safest title one can obtain; the most complete ownership of real estate.

Abstracter's Certificate
A certificate contained in an abstract which shows the time period and the scope of the search of the public records done by the abstracter.

Abstract of Title
A written summary of all succeeding owners, together with a statement of all liens or encumbrances affecting the property.

Agent
One who represents another from whom he has been given authority, i.e., realtor or lawyer.

American Institute of Real Estate Appraisers
A professional institute to promote the quality of the appraisal industry. Refer to the Yellow Pages.

American Land Title Association
An organization of title insurance companies. Refer to the Yellow Pages.

Closing Statement
An accounting of funds in a real estate sale, computed by a realtor or lawyer, showing the obligations of the buyer and the seller.

Cloud on the Title
A claim, encumbrance, judgment, or dower interest which, if valid, would affect or impair the owner's title.

Condominium Ownership
Individual ownership of residential units combined with joint ownership of common areas.

Convey
To transfer title to property.

Conveyance
The means by which title to real estate is transferred from seller to buyer.

Cooperative Apartment
Also called a stock cooperative—a structure of two or more units in which the right to occupy one of the units is obtained by buying a share in the corporation which owns the building.

Covenant

An agreement between two or more persons by deed whereby one of the parties promises the performance or nonperformance of certain acts, or that a given state of things does or does not exist.

Deed

A written legal agreement by which real estate is transferred.

Default

The nonperformance of a duty as stated in a contract, or failure to meet an obligation when due.

Dower

The right which a wife or husband has to her or his spouse's real estate.

Earnest Money (Down Payment or Binder)

A partial payment made by a buyer of real estate as evidence of good faith.

Easement

The right or privilege one has in the land of another, such as a right of way for a sidewalk, driveway, sewer, or power line.

Encroachment

A building, part of a building or obstruction which intrudes upon, invades, or trespasses upon the property of another.

Encumbrance

A lien or claim attached to and binding upon real estate, such as a judgment, unpaid tax, or an easement.

Fee Simple
The largest estate or ownership in real estate; it is free from all conditions or encumbrances.

Free and Clear
Real property against which there are no liens.

General Warranty*
A covenant in the deed whereby the grantor (seller) agrees to protect the grantee (buyer) against the claims of the world.

Land Contract
A contract to purchase real estate on an installment basis; upon payment of the last installment, the deed is delivered to the buyer.

Legal Description
A description recognized by law, which is sufficient to locate and identify the property.

Lien
A claim which one person has upon the property of another as security for a debt, such as judgments, mortgages, or taxes.

Market Price
The highest price which a buyer would pay, and the lowest price a seller would accept.

Marketable Title
A title that a court of law could make a buyer accept; it is free from all encumbrances.

---

*A buyer's best protection!

Metes and Bounds
A description in a deed of the land location, in which the boundaries are defined by directions and distances.

Original Cost
The purchase price of property paid by the present owner.

Pro Rate
To divide in proportionate shares, such as taxes.

Purchase Contract
A written agreement in which the buyer agrees to buy certain real estate and the seller agrees to sell upon terms and conditions set forth therein.

Recording
Filing documents affecting real property as a matter of public record. Usually filed at the county recorder's office.

Restriction
A clause in the deed to control the use of the land, e.g., the lot must be at least 5,000 square feet in area.

Stock Cooperative
See Cooperative Apartment.

Survey
The process by which a parcel of land is measured and its area and boundaries determined.

"Time is of the Essence"
Clause used in contracts to bind one party to perfor-

mance at or by a specified time in order to bind the other party to performance.

Title
Evidence of ownership of real estate.

Title Insurance
A policy of insurance which insures the buyer for any loss sustained by reason of defects in the real estate title. The policy is usually for the price of the home.

Torrens Title
A system by which title to land is registered with a registrar of land titles instead of being recorded.

Trust Deed
See Deed.

Warranty Deed
A deed used in many states to convey fee title to property.

These are the most frequently used terms and phrases. If a different term or phrase is used during the purchase procedure, do not hesitate to ask its meaning and/or application.

Now refer to the Home Search section, page 7.

2
HOME SEARCH

Perhaps these suggestions will be of assistance:

CHOOSE your neighborhood for proximity to work, schools, transportation, parks/playgrounds/sports centers, shopping, and entertainment and cultural facilities.

REFER to the Community and Neighborhood checklist, page 19, for additional neighborhood considerations.

CONSULT with established realtors who are active in the areas in which you are interested.

CHECK local newspapers and community "Homes for Sale" magazines.

DRIVE THROUGH potential neighborhoods, look for realtor signs, and signs "For Sale by Owner."

OTHER POSSIBILITIES Visit the court house and ask about probate sales (estates), sheriff's sales (foreclosures), and tax deeds (nonpayment of taxes).

QUESTION anyone in the neighborhood you are considering. Are they satisfied with the schools, the local government, etc?

Now refer to the Home Inspection checklist, page 9.

3

HOME INSPECTION

NOTE

This inspection applies to either a house or condominium; however, it is not necessary to check items having to do with wear or replacement when inspecting a new house or a new condominium.

We have listed some omissions, flaws, and defects that could be overlooked and we suggest that you obtain and use the following tools and aids: tape measure—pocket compass—flashlight.

Check either the ALERT or OK box for each item—then you will be sure that these important items have been considered!

LIVABILITY FEATURES

ALERT   **OK**

☐   ☐   **ROOMS:** Will the room size accommodate your furniture? (Use the tape measure.)

☐   ☐   **TRAFFIC PATTERN:** Visualize how your family would move through the home. Will the dining and/or living room be used as a hallway? Where would the children enter and how close to a bathroom? Traffic to and from the garage and basement? Separation of adult entertainment, children's play and sleeping areas?

☐   ☐   **BATHROOMS:** Are there enough facilities for the family?

☐   ☐   **MASTER BEDROOM:** Does it afford privacy? Is there a buffer, such as a hall, closet, or bathroom between the master bedroom walls and adjoining rooms?

☐   ☐   **STORAGE SPACE:** Is there adequate closet and storage space in the house, garage, etc.?

☐   ☐   **KITCHEN:** Convenient work area? Adequate cabinet and storage space? Dining area?

☐   ☐   **BASEMENT:** Adequate for your use? Clean, dry, airy? If the laundry is in the basement, is there a possibility of remodeling for this use upstairs?

ALERT OK

☐ ☐ **OUTLOOK FROM WINDOWS:** If the view is wooded and leafy now, what will the view be when the leaves fall?

☐ ☐ **COMPASS ORIENTATION:** Where does the sun rise and set? Will the patio or entertainment areas be in the shade when you prefer? Will you have sun in the windows and rooms when you prefer? (Use the pocket compass.)

☐ ☐ **LOT (YARD):** Is it adequate for your needs? Is there a play area for children?

☐ ☐ **OTHER OBSERVATIONS:** If you find something in addition to the points above that "alerts" you, check this ALERT box and list the item under "Notes" on page 16.

CLOSE EXAMINATION

You may choose to conduct this close examination on your second visit to the home.

LOOK CLOSELY: cracks, flaws, defects, or worn-out areas very often are not noticeable from only a few feet away.

OPEN—CLOSE—PUSH ASIDE—LOOK INTO—LOOK UNDER—OPERATE EVERYTHING!

(For instance, a scatter-rug in front of a fireplace may be covering a hole burned in the carpet underneath—a cutting board on a cabinet top may cover a blemish.)

____ ALERT ____

Do not be surprised later. Be inquisitive now! Ask the sales agent and/or the seller if there are any known defects that have not been corrected. The old principle of *caveat emptor* (buyer beware) is still alive in some areas; however, there is a growing trend to place responsibility and liability on the sales agent and the seller. There are precautions that you can take later on in the buying process, see page 30, Disclosure Checklist and Inspections Contingency.

Determine how much it will cost to repair, refinish, caulk, paint, replace, and/or install the following items. These additional costs would have to be reflected in your offering price.

ALERT   OK

☐   ☐   **CENTRAL AIR CONDITIONING:** If not equipped, consider the cost of installation.

☐   ☐   **STORM DOORS/WINDOWS:** Needed to conserve energy—expensive to install! Make sure that all storm doors and windows are accounted for.

☐   ☐   **ATTIC INSULATION:** Needed to conserve energy—should have 10- to 14-inch thickness and should have an efficiency rating between R22 and R30.

ALERT   OK

☐   ☐ **FURNACE / AIR CONDITIONER / WATER HEATER:** Are they in good shape? What are their ages?

☐   ☐ **UTILITY COSTS:** Ask to see the heating and electric bills for the past 12 months. Would the costs be within your budget?

☐   ☐ **KITCHEN CABINETS:** Check the condition. These are expensive to refinish or to replace!

☐   ☐ **PORCELAIN:** Check for cracks/chips in sinks or tubs. Expensive to replace.

☐   ☐ **CARPETING / DRAPES / BLINDS / SHADES:** Would these need replacement?

☐   ☐ **CERAMIC TILES:** Floors and walls— if cracked, they would be difficult to match.

☐   ☐ **WALLPAPER / PAINTED WALLS / CEILINGS / INTERIOR TRIM:** Is refinishing necessary?

☐   ☐ **LINOLEUM / TILE / HARDWOOD:** In need of replacement?

☐   ☐ **BASEMENT:** A wet or damp basement will have a musty odor. Loose tiles or water spots on floors or walls could signal leaks! If the basement is freshly painted, be suspicious and investigate.

ALERT   OK

☐   ☐   **LOT (YARD):** If there is a hillside involved, the possibility of landslide exists. Is there any history or evidence of landfill? A soil test may be necessary.

☐   ☐   **ROOF:** If asphalt shingle, turned-up edges indicate need for replacement. A normal life is 15 to 17 years. Wood shakes, slate, and tile in good condition will give years of service.

☐   ☐   **GUTTERS AND DOWNSPOUTS:** Is repair or replacement necessary?

☐   ☐   **WINDOWS / DOORS / SIDING AND SHUTTERS:** Is repair or replacement necessary?

☐   ☐   **PORCH / PATIO / DECK:** Is repair or replacement necessary?

☐   ☐   **DRIVEWAYS / SIDEWALKS:** Is repair or replacement of these necessary?

☐   ☐   **INCLUDED IN THE SALE:** Go through the house or condominium with the seller and make a list on page 17 of everything that will be included in the sale, such as refrigerator, range/oven, drapes, fixtures, mirrors, etc. (NOTE: This inventory should be included in your purchase contract!)

ALERT   OK

☐   ☐   **OTHER OBSERVATIONS:** If you find
something in addition to the points above
that "alerts" you, check this ALERT box
and list the item under "Notes" on page
16.

**Now refer to the Community and Neighborhood
checklist on page 19.**

NOTES

Before you proceed with the purchase, obtain a satisfactory answer for any item you have listed below and for any ALERT boxes checked.

_____

_____

_____

_____

_____

_____

_____

_____

_____

_____

_____

_____

_____

_____

_____

_____

_____

_____

_____

INCLUDED IN THE SALE
INVENTORY (see page 14)

This list of items should be included in your purchase contract. Insert in the space provided or attach as an addendum.

_____

_____

_____

_____

_____

_____

_____

_____

_____

_____

_____

_____

_____

_____

_____

_____

_____

4

THE COMMUNITY AND NEIGHBORHOOD

Investigate these items now and save possible irritation, disappointment, and inconvenience.

Check either the ALERT or OK box for each item—then you will be sure that these important items have been considered.

ALERT   OK

☐   ☐   **OVERALL APPEARANCE:** Streets in good repair, homes neat and well maintained?

☐   ☐   **SIZE AND PRICE OF NEIGHBORING HOMES:** The larger, more expensive house or condominium very often does not retain its resale value as well as the more moderately priced unit.

☐   ☐   **AGE OF NEIGHBORING FAMILIES, CHILDREN:** Will your children have playmates?

ALERT   OK

☐   ☐   **SCHOOL   DISTRICT:** School   bus route and nearest stop?

☐   ☐   **PUBLIC   TRANSPORTATION:** Available if needed?

☐   ☐   **ADEQUATE   SERVICES:** Fire, police, waste collection? Which fire district? Are these services included in your taxes or charged separately?

☐   ☐   **LOCATION   OF   NEAREST   FIRE HYDRANT:** Distance can affect fire insurance premiums.

☐   ☐   **WATER AND SEWER SYSTEMS:** Are they adequate? Is there a sewer assessment charge with the water bill? Is the water drinkable? Is it municipal or well water?

☐   ☐   **TELEPHONE   EXCHANGE:** Will your calls be mostly local or long distance?

☐   ☐   **CABLE TV:** Is it available in your area?

☐   ☐   **MEDICAL   FACILITIES:** Physician, dentist, hospital, life squad?

☐   ☐   **SHOPPING FACILITIES / PLAYFIELDS / CHURCHES:** Are they easily accessible?

☐   ☐   **LIGHTS:** Excessive, intruding lights from nearby parking lots, schools, etc.? Drive by at night to check.

ALERT   OK

☐   ☐   **NOISE:** From nearby expressways, highways, manufacturing facilities? Check at various times of the day and night.

☐   ☐   **UNPLEASANT ODORS:** Check prevailing winds for possible unpleasant odors from streams, sewers, factories, etc.

☐   ☐   **POWER LINES:** Possible TV and radio interference. Danger—high voltage lines and transformers may pose health hazards! Check with Power Company.

☐   ☐   **FLOODPLAIN:** History of flooding and/or of water backup?

☐   ☐   **STREET DEDICATION:** Make sure that the street or roadway has been "dedicated" to the community and will be maintained by them.

☐   ☐   **OTHER OBSERVATIONS:** If you find something in addition to the points above that "alerts" you, check this ALERT box and list the item under "Notes" on page 24.

RECORDS RESEARCH

Visit the county court house for the following information. (Ask the clerk for assistance.)

ALERT   OK

☐   ☐   **APPRAISED VALUE:** Look up the combined appraised value of the home and land that municipalities usually appraise, for taxing purposes, at one third of the market value. Multiplying this combined appraised value by three will give you an approximate market value. Is the asking price of the home too high compared to the appraisal?

☐   ☐   **LAST SELLING PRICE:** You can also determine what the present owner paid for this property. This information can guide you in the amount you will offer. (Check the transfer files—ask for help!)

☐   ☐   **REAL ESTATE TAX:** What will the total real estate taxes be? Are they within your budget? (NOTE: After you buy, contact the office of Tax Appraisals. Some municipalities will reduce your taxes periodically based upon depreciation.)

☐   ☐   **INCOME TAX:** Is there a community income tax? If so, is it within your budget?

ALERT OK

☐ ☐ **ORDINANCES:** What are the community ordinances regarding control of fences, pets, animals, unattached sheds/barns, antenna towers, outside storage (boats, trailers, motor homes, etc.)? You may be in favor of some of these, or you may resent a boat being parked in your neighbor's driveway all winter.

☐ ☐ **UNDEVELOPED LOTS OR LAND:** If this situation is adjoining or nearby the property you are considering, how is this land zoned? If it is zoned other than residentially, future development may reduce the value of your property.

☐ ☐ **DEED RESTRICTIONS:** Check the deed restrictions (if any) on the home and lot you are considering. Are these good or bad for you?

☐ ☐ **OTHER OBSERVATIONS:** If you find something in addition to the points above that "alerts" you, check this ALERT box and list the item under "Notes" on page 24.

NOTES

Before you proceed with this purchase, obtain satisfactory answers for any item you have listed below and for any ALERT boxes checked.

_____

_____

_____

_____

_____

_____

_____

_____

_____

_____

_____

_____

_____

_____

_____

_____

_____

_____

This Is a Good Time for a Second Visit to the Home and Neighborhood

It is difficult to absorb everything in just one visit. A second inspection may point out problems originally missed.

Now you are ready to make an offer. Refer to Negotiating Price and the Purchase Contract checklists, page 27.

5
NEGOTIATING PRICE AND THE PURCHASE CONTRACT

NEGOTIATING PRICE

CHECK the court house for the last selling price. (Ask the clerk for assistance.)

COMPARE recent selling prices for comparable homes. (Your realtor can supply this information.)

APPRAISE: Have a professional appraiser suggest value. (Check Yellow Pages under Real Estate Appraisers.)

ALLOW a fair appreciation factor for the seller.

COMPUTE the real estate commission the seller must pay.

DEDUCT the cost of repairs and/or replacements that you will be required to make immediately.

NOTE

The seller usually expects to reduce the asking price. *Negotiate! Counteroffer!* **Factors to consider: appraisal; original cost; appreciation; selling expenses; reasonable profit; comparable sales.**

THE PURCHASE CONTRACT

Purchase contracts differ in form and wording; therefore it is recommended that you consult a lawyer. The following recommendations and suggestions are for your consideration and are not to be taken as legal advice:

- Read all of the contract, and question anything that you do not understand.
- If any of the clauses, phrases, or contingencies that follow are not in your contract, write in or add them to the end of the contract as an addendum.
- Never sign a contract, papers, or promissory note until you are sure of all the conditions.

Check the ALERT box or the OK box for each of the following items. Then you can be sure that all of the clauses have been considered.

PRICE AND TERMS CLAUSE

The buyer hereby agrees to pay $ _____ (purchase price) for the real estate as follows:

ALERT   OK

☐   ☐   **DOWN PAYMENT:** $ _____ of these funds are to apply towards the purchase price and are to be held in escrow until the closing. If this offer is not accepted by the seller, if the seller should default in the performance of the contract, or if the buyer should terminate this contract as provided for by the contingency clauses herein, the down payment shall be returned to the buyer.

☐   ☐   **BUYER DEFAULT CLAUSE:** If this clause is in the purchase contract, delete any part of it that refers to the seller suing for damages, full purchase price, specific performance, or strict foreclosure. (If you should default, your liability would be limited to your down payment only.)

FINANCING CONTINGENCY CLAUSE

ALERT   OK

☐   ☐   **FINANCING CONTINGENCY:** This contract is contingent upon the buyer's ability to obtain, within 45 days, a loan of $ _____ at the rate of _____ percent for a term of _____ years.

NOTE _____

If you cannot obtain suitable financing, you can get out of the contract, or you can agree to other suitable terms and proceed with the closing. It is your option!

CONTINGENCY INSPECTIONS CLAUSE

ALERT   OK

☐   ☐   **DISCLOSURE CHECKLIST:** If available, have the seller sign a disclosure checklist, which many real estate agents now use for their protection. Also check on the availability of a one-year home warranty policy. (Ask your realtor.) *In addition, make sure that you insert the following inspections contingency into the purchase contract.*

☐   ☐   **INSPECTIONS   CONTINGENCY:** This contract is contingent upon the buyer performing or obtaining at his/her cost and to his/her complete satisfaction the following inspections: Termite, radon gas, formaldehyde gas, asbestos, electrical, structural, and all mechanical systems. These inspections are to be completed within 45 days.

NOTE _____

Insert THE CONTINGENCY CLAUSE into the purchase contract. If space is limited, add this clause as an addendum to the purchase contract.

Use the Contingency Home Inspection checklists when these inspections are made.

INCLUDED IN THE SALE CLAUSE

ALERT   OK

☐   ☐   Insert into the purchase contract the "inventory" of items that you and the seller agreed to include in the sale price! (See the Home Inspection checklist on page 14.)

CONVEYANCE AND CLOSING CLAUSE

ALERT   OK

☐   ☐   Seller shall be responsible for pro-rated taxes at the time of closing, deed preparation, transfer taxes, real estate commission and shall convey to the buyer a *marketable title**, *free and clear**, in *fee simple**, by *Deed of General Warranty**, or *Abstracter's Certificate of Title**, or *Certificate of Title**, or *Torrens Title**, or as local custom may dictate.

_____

*See definitions on pages 1–6, for italicized terms.

____ ALERT ____

It is our strong recommendation that you obtain title insurance—it is worth the cost.

NOTE _____

Make sure that you receive a copy of the Closing Statement and other related documents

CONDITIONS OF IMPROVEMENTS CLAUSE

ALERT   OK

☐   ☐   The seller agrees that, on possession, the real estate shall be in the same condition as it is on the date of this offer, except for ordinary wear and damage from insurable perils.

____ ALERT ____

Danger! Regulations and laws differ by state as to where responsibility lies in the event of fire or extended damages that occur from the date of the purchase to the closing date. Be safe. Ask your insurance agent for a binder on the property from the date of the purchase to the closing date. The binder would convert to a standard policy at that time.

RELEASE OF DOWER

ALERT   OK

☐   ☐   **SIGNATURES:** Obtain the signatures of all owners on the purchase contract and the deed. In the case of husband and wife or co-owners, both signatures are needed for "release of dower." In the case of more than two owners, signatures of all parties are necessary.

☐   ☐   **OTHER OBSERVATIONS:** If you find something in addition to the points above that "alerts" you, check this ALERT box and list the item under "Notes" below.

SUMMARY: You now have 45 days to obtain the financing that you need and to perform the "Contingency Home Inspection." If you cannot obtain suitable financing or the home inspection is not satisfactory, you may, because of the purchase contract contingency clauses, declare the contract null and void, and have your down payment returned.

Now refer to the Contingency Home Inspection checklist on page 35. You are checking for defects that determine if you will or will not buy this particular house or condominium.

NOTES

Before you proceed with the purchase, obtain satisfactory answers for any item you have listed below and for any ALERT boxes checked.

_____

_____

_____

_____

_____

_____

_____

_____

_____

_____

_____

_____

_____

_____

_____

_____

_____

_____

_____

_____

_____

_____

6
CONTINGENCY HOME INSPECTION

NEW HOUSE OR NEW CONDOMINIUM

When buying a new home or a new condominium, it is not necessary to check items having to do with wear, repair and/or replacement; however, be alert and insist upon a written builder's warranty covering all exterior and interior structural components—plumbing, heating and electrical systems, all concrete steps, porches, driveways, walks, floors, etc. Also be sure to obtain copies of the manufacturers' warranties covering all mechanical equipment, e.g., furnace, air conditioner, heat pump, water heater, refrigerator, range/oven, dishwasher, compactor, garage door opener, fans, etc. You should receive a copy of the roofing manufacturer's warranty.

ALERT   OK

☐   ☐   **BUILDER'S WARRANTY:** Normally 1 year.

☐   ☐   **MANUFACTURER'S WARRANTY:** Normally 1 year.

☐   ☐   **ROOFING MATERIAL WARRANTY:** Normally 20 years.

PREVIOUSLY OWNED HOUSE OR CONDOMINIUM

The following inspections are to be accomplished as a follow-up to the Contingency Clause that you had inserted in your purchase contract. These inspections can be made by you and/or a qualified building inspector. It is recommended that you hire a professional. Check the Yellow Pages under "Building Inspectors," or ask your realtor. (**NOTE: These inspectors may not be certified, licensed or bonded, so check references.**)

If you do the inspections personally, take along the following aids—flashlight, ¼-inch screwdriver, three-foot level, and plug-in night-light.

Checklist

ALERT   OK

☐   ☐   **TERMITE INSPECTION**

☐   ☐   **RADON INSPECTION**

☐   ☐   **FOAM INSULATION**

ALERT	OK	
☐	☐	**PARTICLE BOARD**
☐	☐	**ASBESTOS INSULATION**

NOTE

See the following for technical information regarding the previous items.

_____ ALERT _____

If any or all of these are discovered, there is reason for alarm—termites can be responsible for *structural damage*—radon, foam insulation, particle board, and asbestos could pose a *definite health hazard*.

TERMITES: A definite possibility of structural damage. Check the Yellow Pages for a professional exterminator. Some will inspect the premises for no charge. (This inspection is not necessary if you are buying a new home.)

RADON is a radioactive gas produced by the decay of uranium in rocks and soil. This gas can seep into a home. Excessive inhalation of this gas can cause lung cancer. A test reading of *4 or more picocuries does pose risk*. (A picocurie is a measure of radiation.)

NOTE

Test Kits and Test Agencies Are Available
For Information Call
Your Local Health Department and/or
Environmental Protection Agency at
1-800-767-7236

FOAM INSULATION used in wall cavities and/or as ceiling insulation. Check attic or crawl space. Remove wall electric outlet plates to check wall cavities.

PARTICLE BOARD: Sometimes used as underlay for carpets and other types of flooring also, used in the manufacture of kitchen cabinets and wall paneling.

ALERT

DANGER! If either foam insulation or particle board is found, there is a possibility of health hazard due to toxic formaldehyde gas fumes.

FORMALDEHYDE
Test Kits and Test Agencies Are Available
For Information Call
Your Local Health Department or
the local 3M Company Sales Office
They will direct you to a distributor of the
Formaldehyde Monitor.

ASBESTOS INSULATION: This is usually only found in homes built before 1950; however, if present, there is risk.

NOTE

Additional information about the dangers of foam insulation, particle board and asbestos can be obtained by writing to:

U.S. Consumer Product Safety Commission
1111 18th Street N.W.
Washington, D.C. 20207

NOTE _____

The issue of danger associated with these products has become controversial—some claim little or no danger; others warn about health hazards. Laws regarding disclosure by builders and real estate salespersons differ by state. We like the old adage—"Be safe, not sorry."

USE YOUR CHECKLISTS

ALERT OK

☐ ☐ **OTHER OBSERVATIONS:** If you find something in addition to the points above that "alerts" you, check this ALERT box and list the item under "Notes" on page 47.

Obtain a satisfactory answer for any ALERT box that you have checked!

ELECTRIC SYSTEM INSPECTION

ALERT OK

☐ ☐ **WALL SWITCHES / OUTLETS AND FIXTURES:** Check the operation and function of each item—interior and exterior! (Use the plug-in night-light.)

☐ ☐ **WIRING:** Determine the use of copper or aluminum wiring by removing several wall outlet plates and also inspecting the main fuse or breaker box.

ALERT

Danger! If aluminum wiring is found, there is a potential fire hazard!

MECHANICAL SYSTEMS INSPECTION

ALERT OK

☐ ☐ **FIREPLACE:** You can check the operation (draw) by burning papers.

☐ ☐ **BATHROOMS:** Flush all toilets, and note flushing and refill action. Run all faucets in sinks, tubs, and showers; note water pressure—strong? Do the drains flow swiftly? Operate exhaust fans and auxiliary heaters.

☐ ☐ **KITCHEN:** Run all faucets—check for water pressure. Do the drains flow swiftly? Run the dishwasher through all cycles. Check the disposal and trash compactor. Operate all the burners on the range (stove). Check full operation of the oven, including the self-cleaning feature. Check the refrigerator, if included in the sale.

☐ ☐ **FANS:** Exhaust or ventilation—kitchen, bathroom, hall, attic, roof or ceiling—check operation and all speed

ALERT OK

settings. Are they vented to the outside? This is necessary for proper function of fans.

☐ ☐ **FURNACE / AIR CONDITIONING SYSTEM / HEAT PUMP / ELEC-TRONIC AIR FILTER / HUMIDI-FIER:** Check all systems completely. Turn on and operate.

☐ ☐ **WATER HEATER:** Check for leaks. Is the size adequate for your family?

☐ ☐ **LAUNDRY:** If washer and dryer are included in the sale, check through all cycles. Is the dryer vented to the outside? Check laundry tub faucet pressure and draining action.

☐ ☐ **BASEMENT / FLOOR / DRAINS:** Check them for fast draining action.

☐ ☐ **GARAGE DOORS / ELECTRIC OPENER:** Check operation. Check all switches and hand-held operating devices.

☐ ☐ **DOOR LOCKS / OPENERS:** Check for full function—do all locks lock?

☐ ☐ **OTHER ITEMS:** Check and operate any mechanical object or system, not mentioned above, included in the sale of the home.

☐ ☐ **WARRANTIES:** Ask the seller for all warranties, and operating and repair manuals.

ALERT OK

☐ ☐ **OTHER OBSERVATIONS:** If you find something in addition to the points above that "alerts" you, check this ALERT box and list the item under "Notes" on page 47.

Obtain a satisfactory answer for any ALERT box that you have checked!

STRUCTURAL EXTERIOR INSPECTION

ALERT OK

☐ ☐ **FOUNDATION:** If you find a deep crack, determine if it goes through the foundation into the basement.

☐ ☐ **DOWNSPOUTS:** These should extend down into the soil pipe or be directed away from the house. If not, runoff water may be undermining the foundation.

☐ ☐ **BRICKWORK:** Check for cracks zigzagging along the brick courses.

☐ ☐ **PORCHES AND DECKS:** Are they level and securely attached to the house?

☐ ☐ **ALIGNMENT:** Walk around the house noting anything out of alignment—roof ridge line, gutters, porch roof, supporting columns, steps, etc.

___ ALERT ___

Danger! If you find any or all of the above structural flaws, there is a distinct possibility of foundation movement. Investigate further!

ALERT   OK

☐   ☐   **ROOF:** Are all shingles or tiles in place. Are all gutters and downspouts in place and fastened securely?

☐   ☐   **SIDEWALKS / DRIVEWAY:** These should be level and firmly supported.

☐   ☐   **SURVEY:** A survey may be necessary if you find reason to doubt the accuracy of the lot boundary lines, or you suspect encroachment (see the Real Estate Terms and Phrases checklist) by the building, a building extension, or driveway, etc. (NOTE: Encroachment may make the title unmarketable.)

STRUCTURAL INTERIOR INSPECTION

ALERT   OK

☐   ☐   **CRACKS AND / OR SAGGING:** Check around all of the doors and windows for signs of cracks in the paper, paint, plaster, or dry wall. (You may have to pull aside the drapes, blinds, or

ALERT   OK

curtains to accomplish this.) Check for sagging doors, crooked doorjambs, or evidence of uneven floors. (Use the three-foot level).

☐   ☐   **BASEMENT / FOUNDATION / WALLS:** Closely inspect for cracks or evidence of water penetration.

☐   ☐   **JACK POST:** This is a post that operates like an automobile jack, telescoping upward to support a beam or joist. It is used to shore up sagging floors or supporting members. It is not a normal construction member.

☐   ☐   **SEPARATION:** Look for cracks, separation between walls, doorjambs, windows, countertops, shower stalls, bathtubs, etc.

ALERT

> Danger! If you find any or all of the above structural flaws, there is a distinct possibility of foundation movement. Investigate further!

ALERT   OK

☐   ☐   **WINDOWS AND DOORS:** Do they all operate properly—unlock and lock? Is any of the glass cracked or missing?

ALERT   OK

☐   ☐   **FLOORS:** Are they level and solid? Do you feel any soft spots in the floors as you walk over them?

☐   ☐   **STAIRS AND STAIR RAILS:** Are these solid and securely fastened?

☐   ☐   **OTHER OBSERVATIONS:** If you find something in addition to the points above that "alerts" you, check this ALERT box and list the item under "Notes" on page 47.

Obtain a satisfactory answer for any ALERT box that you have checked!

OPTIONS AVAILABLE

If you and / or your agent have found a major defect in the home, you have the following options open to you.

1) After determining the costs for replacement and / or repair of the defect, you can, upon agreement with the seller, deduct these costs from the selling price. Proceed with the closing and then at a later date make the repairs or replacement yourself.
2) You can have the seller make the necessary repairs and/or replacements, then, upon another inspection of these items, you can proceed to obtain financing.

3) You can, under the contract contingency clause, declare the contract null and void and get your down payment returned.
4) If you did not find any hazards or defects, you can attempt to procure ''satisfactory financing'' as stipulated in your Finance Contingency Clause.

Now refer to Financing Terms and Phrases, page 49, and then to the Mortgage Loan Application checklist, page 59.

NOTES

Before you proceed, obta
to any ALERT boxes you m
any items you may have lis

_____
_____
_____
_____
_____
_____
_____
_____
_____
_____
_____
_____
_____
_____
_____
_____
_____
_____
_____

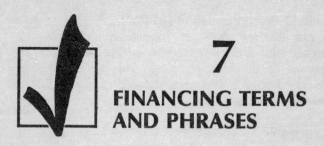

7
FINANCING TERMS AND PHRASES

It is suggested that you become familiar with these terms and phrases that are found in real estate documents and referred to by realtors and lawyers:

Acceleration Clause
A clause used in an installment note and mortgage (or deed of trust), which gives the lender the right to demand payment in full upon the happening of certain events such as failure to pay an installment by a certain date, the change of ownership without the lender's consent, destruction of the property, or other events which might endanger the security of the loan.

Alienation Clause
See Due-on-Sale Clause.

Amortization
Gradual repayment of a loan through a predetermined schedule of payments of principal and interest. At the

maturity of the loan, both principal and interest are completely paid.

Annual Percentage Rate (APR)
A rate that represents the total finance charges—interest, loan fees, points, etc.—expressed as a percentage of the loan principal. This figure must be disclosed to a borrower under the federal Truth in Lending Law.

Assumable Mortgage
The purchaser takes ownership to real estate encumbered by an existing mortgage and assumes responsibility as the guarantor for the unpaid balance of the mortgage.

Balloon Payment
The final payment on a loan, usually substantially larger than previous payments, which repays the loan in full.

Cap
An arbitrary limit set on the rate of an adjustable rate mortgage.

Certificate of Reasonable Value (CRV)
A document (appraisal) issued by the Veterans Administration establishing their opinion of the maximum value.

Closing Costs (Settlement Costs)
Expenses, such as loan, title, attorney fees, etc., incurred in a real estate transaction. These costs are paid at the consummation of the transaction.

Collateral
Assets pledged as security for repayment of a loan.

Debt Service
The amount of money needed to meet the principal and interest payments on an amortized loan.

Deed of Trust
Used in some states like a mortgage. In a mortgage transaction, there are usually two parties, the mortgagor and the mortgagee. In the deed of trust, there are three parties—the *borrower* executes the deed of trust to a third party (*trustee*), who holds for the *owner-seller*.

Due-on-Sale Clause
A form of acceleration clause that calls due, at the lender's option, the entire outstanding balance of a loan upon the sale or transfer of a property. This is used by lenders primarily as a means of restricting either a loan assumption or sale of a property without the lender's approval. Several states have ruled against the enforceability of this clause.

Effective Rate
The actual interest paid on a loan, regardless of the stated contract rate.

Equity
The difference between a property's market value and the amount of all mortgages against the property. Refers to an owner's interest in a property.

Escalation Clause

A provision in a mortgage agreement that allows the contract interest rate to increase based upon a prescribed schedule or a change in an economic index.

Escrow

The holding of monies and/or documents by a disinterested third-party agent under the terms and conditions of the escrow instructions. When these terms are satisfied, the funds or documents are delivered.

Indexing

Adjusting the interest rate on a loan in accordance with the movements of an index or economic indicator, i.e., the U.S. Treasury bill rate or the consumer price index.

Interim Financing

Temporary financing, usually for construction.

Kicker

Any benefit or bonus to a lender, such as extra interest or participation in equity or profits, over and above ordinary interest receipts.

Land Contract

An arrangement of seller financing whereby a buyer takes possession of a property and makes installment payments to the seller until the purchase price is completely paid, or until the buyer is able to obtain alternate financing. Often legal title to the property does not pass to the buyer until all provisions of the contract are fulfilled or until a specified portion of the purchase price is paid.

Leverage
The use of borrowed money to increase the size of a cash investment and therefore its returns. The larger the loan is in relation to the equity, the greater is the leverage.

Loan-to-Value Ratio
The ratio of the mortgage loan (amount borrowed) on the property to the appraised value (selling price). For example, a $100,000 home with a mortgage loan of $80,000 would have a loan to value ratio of 80 percent.

Maturity
The time at which a mortgage note or other debt investment becomes due and payable.

Mortgage
A legal document that pledges property as security for the payment of a debt or performance of an obligation.

Mortgage (First)
The mortgage on a property that has priority in right or claim, as determined by the time of recording, over any other mortgages on the property.

Mortgage (Second)
A mortgage that is second or subordinate in priority to an existing mortgage on the same property. Used primarily to fill a gap between a buyer's down payment and the amount of a new first mortgage.

Mortgage Banker
A company dealing only in mortgages—usually offering very competitive interest rates.

Mortgage Deed of Trust
A pledge of real property to secure a debt. This term means the same thing as mortgage.

Mortgage Insurance Premium (MIP)
Payments made by a borrower for mortgage insurance to either the FHA or a private mortgage insurance company (*see* Private Mortgage Insurance).

Mortgagee
A lender who holds a mortgage as security for repayment of a debt.

Mortgagor
A borrower of money (buyer) who gives a mortgage as security.

Note
A document signed by a borrower that states the loan amount, the interest rate, the term and method of repayment, and a promise to repay the loan amount. A note is written evidence of a debt.

Origination Fee
A fee charged by a lender to cover initial loan expenses, such as credit inspection, appraisal fee, loan application processing, and other administrative costs.

Package Mortgage
A loan that finances the purchase of real estate and related personal property—appliances and other home accessories—at the same time.

PITI
The elements that commonly make up a borrower's payment on an amortized loan: principal, interest, taxes, and insurance.

Point
One percent of the principal of a loan. Points are loan fees charged by lenders to increase the yields on below-market interest rate loans to competitive levels, and are paid when the loan is closed. Also called discount points.

Prepaid Expenses
The initial deposit (installment payment) at the time of closing for mortgage insurance premiums and/or taxes, and the following monthly installment payments paid to the lender to cover these expenses. (NOTE: These amounts would be added to your monthly principal and interest payments.)

Prepayment Penalty
A fee paid to the mortgagee as a result of the mortgagor's paying off the mortgage before it has become due.

Prepayment Privilege
The right given a purchaser to pay all or part of a debt (mortgage) prior to its maturity.

Principal
The total amount of a mortgage debt. The amount upon which the interest is computed.

Private Mortgage Insurance (PMI)

Insurance provided by a private company (rather than the FHA) that protects the lender against loss caused by a borrower's default. The borrower, however, pays the premium for the insurance.

Qualify

Having sufficient financial capability to afford the payments on a loan. Depending upon the amount of the loan and the interest rate, lenders usually require that borrowers meet specified income requirements.

Recourse

The right of a holder of a note secured by a mortgage or deed of trust to look personally to the borrower for payment, not just the property.

RESPA—Real Estate Settlement Procedures Act

A federal law calling for uniform closing statements to be given to the buyer and the seller. This statement will reflect the various charges that are the responsibility of the buyer or the seller.

Truth in Lending Statement

The government requires that this statement be given to anyone who applies for a home loan from any lending institution. This statement will reveal the annual percentage rate (APR) as well as the Total Pay Out over the life of the loan.

Usury

The charging of an interest rate on a loan that is greater than the rate permitted by law.

Variable Rate
A mortgage loan rate that increases or decreases directly with fluctuations of an index beyond the control of the lender.

Vendor Lien
Used in some states like a mortgage. The vendor lien comes about when the vendor/seller has conveyed title of real estate to a vendee/buyer but has not received the full purchase price.

Without Recourse
See Recourse.

Now refer to the Mortgage Loan Application checklist on page 59.

Now refer to the Mortgage Loan Application checklist on page 59.

NOTE
You will have to complete this loan application checklist before you apply to the lending institutions. The loan officers will need this information to qualify you for a loan.

8
MORTGAGE LOAN APPLICATION CHECKLIST

This checklist is designed to help you prepare for the mortgage loan interview. It will save you time if you are fully prepared in advance.

WHERE TO GO FOR A MORTGAGE LOAN

Full service banks, savings and loans (thrifts), mortgage bankers, life insurance companies, and your employer are all possible sources of loans

You might try a computer search for mortgage financing. This is the use of a computer network to obtain a list of competitive home mortgages and terms available from local and area lending institutions. Check your Real Estate Board, realtor, Home Builders Association, or telephone directory.

PERSONAL DEMEANOR

• Dress neatly and conservatively.
• Be confident, cooperative, and sincere.
• Answer all questions fully and honestly.

PREPARATION

Be prepared to answer the following questions and
check each item as you compile the information:

Personal Information

How long have you lived at your

        present address?   _____

        previous address?   _____

How long have you been employed at
your

        present job?   _____

        previous job?   _____

Present employer? _____

Social security number? _____

Credit references—list all of your established credit
references, such as installment loans and credit cards
(Visa, American Express, MasterCard, gasoline cards,
and department store cards). Show account numbers.
Current and previous years' W-2 wage and tax forms
for yourself and spouse.

Assets and Income

A) Present yearly income? $ _____

Bank accounts/credit union accounts, etc. If more than one, list separately along with the account number and enter totals. Current balances? $ _____

B) Total yearly interest income? $ _____

Investments—money market accounts, stocks, bonds, IRA's, real estate, etc. If more than one, list separately along with the account number and enter totals. Current balances? $ _____

Total yearly income (interest/dividends/rents: Add lines A and B). $ _____

Insurance-cash surrender value of all policies? (Not face value.) $ _____

Other assets—written appraisals and/or insurance policies covering expensive jewelry, antiques, etc. Total value? $ _____

Personal property worth—current estimated value of your furniture, clothing, appliances, etc? (Do not include automobiles, insured jewelry, or antiques, etc.) Be conservative! (Used items such as those above do not bring a high price.) $ _____

Automobiles—fully paid for—no loan. Estimated value? $ _____

Total. $ _____

Liabilities and Expenses

Loans/notes—automobiles, furniture, appliances, campers, boats, etc. If more than one, list separately and enter totals.
    Original amounts of loans? $ _____
    Remaining balances? $ _____

A) Total monthly payments? $ _____
Mortgages—investment real estate, vacation home, etc. If more than one, list separately and enter totals.
    Original mortgages? $ _____

    Remaining balances? $ _____

B) Total monthly payments? $ _____

Insurance premiums—life, health, automobile, liability, home (comprehensive), etc. If more than one, list separately and enter totals.
C) Total monthly premiums? $ _____

D) Rent payments—total monthly? $ _____

E) Home mortgage payments—total monthly? $ _____

F) Utilities—average monthly total for utilities? $ _____

G) Other monthly payments? (In addition to those above.) $ _____

Total of all monthly payments. (Add lines A–G.) $ _____

H) Multiply total monthly payments by 12 for *total yearly payments*. $ _____

I) Taxes—real estate, income, etc. List
and enter individual totals. Total taxes? $ _____
Grand total of fixed yearly payments.
(Add lines H and I.) $ _____

Additional Mortgage Loan Information

Use this sheet to list your multiple credit references,
credit cards, bank accounts, money market accounts,
stocks, bonds, etc. *List all account numbers.*

_____

_____

_____

_____

_____

_____

_____

_____

_____

_____

_____

_____

_____

_____

_____

_____

_____

_____

_____

_____

_____

_____

_____

_____

_____

_____

_____

_____

_____

The loan officer will be using your Mortgage Loan Application information to compute your net worth and your ability to carry monthly expenses plus the additional costs of this new mortgage loan. It is important that this information be accurate and complete.

RECOMMENDATION: Make several copies of your Mortgage Loan Application checklist. You should shop around and compare several lending institutions. If your loan application should be turned down, ask the loan officer why. It is your right to know.

You are now ready to obtain your financing. Refer to 32 Ways to Finance Your Home Purchase, page 67.

9

32 WAYS TO FINANCE YOUR HOME PURCHASE

SHOPPING FOR A LOAN BARGAIN

There are many different lending institutions out there and each one is offering a different interest rate, with a different number of points on different size loans. The numbers are different if you are considering a fixed rate or an ARM (adjustable rate mortgage).

<u>Compare</u>

Do not hesitate to obtain proposals from several lending institutions. They are in the business and expect to compete.

ALERT

Creative financing plans do fulfill a need; however, their lower rates in the beginning may result in unbearable rates at a later date. Lending institutions are required by law to give you a *Truth in Lending Statement* that will reveal the annual percentage rate (APR) and the Total Pay Out for the loan.

CHECK YOUR LOAN FOR THE FOLLOWING CLAUSES, BE POSITIVE THAT YOU UNDERSTAND THEM. ASK QUESTIONS!

Checklist

ALERT   OK

☐   ☐   **ACCELERATION CLAUSE?**

☐   ☐   **RECOURSE CLAUSE?**

☐   ☐   **INTEREST CAP (ARM)?**

☐   ☐   **BALLOON CLAUSE?**

☐   ☐   **PREPAYMENT PENALTY?**

☐   ☐   **PREPAYMENT PRIVILEGE?**

Option to Save Money

While shopping for a loan, keep this in mind. You can, by use of accelerated payments, save thousands of dollars and reduce the term of your mortgage. This is accomplished by adding $25 or $50 dollars monthly to your scheduled payment. If you find that you are unable to pay this accelerated amount, you simply drop back to your scheduled payment. Discuss this with your loan officer.

ALERT

Be sure that your loan has prepayment privilege and does not have prepayment penalty. Also, keep a record of all accelerated payments made.

Another option: You might consider a 15- or 20-year amortization instead of the standard 30-year fixed-rate mortgage.

Here are some of the ways you can finance your home:

Adjustable Rate Mortgage Loan (ARM)

Mortgage loans under which the interest rate is periodically adjusted to more closely coincide with current rates. The term is either 1 year or 3 years. The interest rate is pegged to Treasury Securities. There should be a cap on incremental interest rate increases as well as a cap on the total interest rate increase over the life of the loan.

Blanket Mortgage

Where the buyer has a high enough equity in other property so that the new loan (mortgage) is used to finance both properties.

Blended-Rate Mortgage or Weighted Average Money Mortgage (WAMM)

A below-market interest rate mortgage that combines into a new loan the outstanding balance of an existing loan and an additional amount of new money; the originator of the loan is usually the lender who holds the existing mortgage. The interest rate on the new loan is the weighted average of the rate on the existing loan and the current market rate on the new loan.

Bridge Loan

A short-term loan on one property that is applied toward the purchase of another prior to the sale of the first property. Used when the buyer needs the proceeds (cash) of a sale before purchasing another property.

Convertible Adjustable Rate Mortgage

This is an adjustable cut-rate, dual-capped mortgage which is heavily discounted up front. The loan carries a 2 percent annual rate increase cap, and a 5-year, life-of-the-loan rate increase limit of 15½ percent. For no additional fee up front, this loan can be converted to a long-term, fixed rate. (NOTE: The advantages to you are that decision making is up to you, the loan is heavily discounted up front, and the conversion option is cost free until you find it advantageous to use it.)

Employer Mortgage Assistance

Many large corporations are now extending mortgage loan assistance to their employees as an added benefit. These loans are usually fixed-rate, below-market 15- and 30-year loans. Check with your employer.

Farmer's Home Administration (FmHA)

An agency within the U.S. Department of Agriculture that provides financing assistance to farmers and rural residents who are unable to obtain financing elsewhere. Housing loans are made either on a direct basis or by private lenders with FmHA guaranty.

Federal Housing Administration (FHA)

An agency under the Department of Housing and Urban Development that insures residential mortgage loans made by private lenders. For this purpose it has well-established structural and loan qualifying standards. FHA-insured loans usually can be obtained with lower down payments and interest rates than other conventional loans. The FHA does not lend money.

Federal National Mortgage Association (FNMA)

A privately owned corporation that purchases and sells primarily FHA and VA loans in the secondary mortgage market. Offers a refinancing program whereby a buyer or homeowner can convert an existing mortgage into a new mortgage with a higher loan-to-value ratio and an interest rate below current market rates.

Fixed-Payment Adjustable Loan Mortgage

This carries a discount rate 2 to 2½ percentage points under the going price for 30-year fixed-payment mortgages. Rates are fixed for 5 years at a time. After 5 years, there are two choices available: 1) you can convert to a standard fixed-rate mortgage for 25 years, or 2) you can get another 5-year fixed rate with payments based upon the average of the last 4 years' rates and the current prevailing rate on 1-year adjustables.

Fixed-Rate Mortgage

A standard for many years. The interest rate remains constant for the life of the loan (mortgage).

Graduated Payment Adjustable Mortgage (GPAM)

A mortgage that combines the features of a graduated payment mortgage (GPM) and an adjustable rate mortgage (ARM). Monthly payments gradually increase during the initial term of the loan, not to exceed ten years, and the loan's interest rate may be adjusted up or down based upon movement of an agreed-upon index.

Graduated Payment Mortgage (GPM)

A fixed-rate mortgage with lower monthly payments during the initial years than are necessary to fully amortize the loan. Payments gradually rise by a set annual percentage during this initial period, after which they remain constant for the remaining life of the loan.

Growing Equity Mortgage (GEM)

A fixed-rate mortgage on which payments are adjusted annually to reflect the rate of change in an index of per capita, disposable, personal income. The annual adjustment is then applied to the previous year's monthly payment and any resulting increase above the loan's initial payment goes entirely toward repayment of the principal.

Howe Financing

Buyers qualify for loans up to 95 percent of the value of the home at initial rates 3 to 4 points below the going market charges for fixed-rate loans. During the next 2 to 3 years, the rate moves up by 1 or 2 points per year until it reaches the "contract" note rate. The contract rate is pegged 1 to 1¼ percent above the Federal Home Loan Mortgage Corporation quote for long-term, fixed-rate mortgages at the date of closing. The Howe concept is intended to either reduce the initial sales price or permit the builders to offer higher amenities without raising the sales price.

Land Contract

Seller finances, buyer takes possession and makes installment payments until full price is paid, or until alternate financing is obtained. (ALERT: Legal title [deed] does not pass to the buyer until full price is paid. Also, watch for a due-on-sale clause in the seller's mortgage.)

Lease
An option or privilege to buy or a mandatory clause to buy.

Life Insurance Companies
The nation's largest life insurance companies are now entering the home mortgage market. They are offering a nationwide network of agents, competitive rates, sophisticated telephone loan application and approval systems. (Check with your insurance company, realtor, etc.)

Loan Assumption
Buyer assumes the seller's mortgage. (ALERT: Watch for a due-on-sale clause in the mortgage—subject to lender's approval.)

100 Percent Loan
Seller refinances up to maximum amount and allows the buyer to purchase for the said amount and assume the loan. (ALERT: Watch for a due-on-sale clause.)

"One, Two, Three" Financing
A method of creative financing by which the buyer (1) assumes the existing loan, (2) secures a second loan from a third party lender, (3) takes a third loan from the seller.

Open Mortgage
A mortgage permitting the mortgagor to borrow additional money under the same mortgage.

Pledged Amount Mortgage (PAM)
A mortgage that calls for all or a portion of a buyer's down payment to be placed in an interest-bearing ac-

count. The account is pledged as additional security for the loan and is used to supplement the loan's payments during the initial years of the loan. A Flexible Loan Insurance Program (FLIP) is one variation of a PAM.

Price Level Adjusted Mortgage (PLAM)

A mortgage on which the outstanding loan balance varies by an adjustment, at the end of each year, of an inflation factor, such as the change in the consumer price index. The loan's interest rate is actually a real rate of interest, i.e., a rate that would exist if there were no inflation.

Purchase Money Mortgage

Seller holds the first mortgage, but the deed (legal title) passes to the buyer.

7/23 Mortgage

This is a seven-year fixed-rate mortgage with payments based upon a 30-year amortization. It includes a 23-year extension with neither reappraisal or credit check. The interest rate is capped at 5 percent (maximum increase). It offers an interest rate below the 30-year fixed rate.

Shared Appreciation Mortgage (SAM)

A mortgage on which a lender charges a below-market interest rate in exchange for an agreed-upon percentage of the secured property's net appreciation. The lender's share of the appreciation, contingent interest, is due when the property is sold or the loan reaches maturity. The lender may refinance the outstanding loan balance along with the contingent interest at maturity.

Shared Equity Purchase (SEP)

A purchase agreement that is essentially a partnership or joint venture between a buyer and a lender or an investor. A substantial portion of the buyer's down payment is provided by an investor who then holds an equity interest in the property and pays a portion of the mortgage expenses. When the property is sold, the investor receives a percentage of the accumulated equity.

Trade-In

Seller accepts buyer's home as full or partial payment. (ALERT: Uses a specifically worded agreement covering price and equity of each home.)

Variable Rate Mortgage (VRM)

A mortgage on which the interest rate is adjusted to reflect changes in a lender's cost of loanable funds. Rate adjustments may be implemented through changes in the payment amount or by extending the loan term.

Veterans Administration (VA)

A federal agency that allows eligible veterans to obtain residential mortgage loans, with little or no down payment, from private lending institutions. The VA guarantees the lender for a specified amount of the loan in the event of default by the borrower.

Wraparound Mortgage

A second mortgage on which a lender, often a seller, lends an amount larger than the existing first mortgage without paying off or disturbing the existing mortgage. The amount of the loan equals the selling price of the property minus the buyer's down payment; the interest rate is usually higher than on the existing mortgage. The wraparound lender continues to make payments on the existing mortgage using the proceeds from the wraparound mortgage.

NOTE

The Federal National Mortgage Association (Fannie Mae), recently announced the establishment of a uniform loan assumption fee to ensure that consumers are not overcharged on the assumption of conventional mortgage loans owned by Fannie Mae. For transfers that require credit approval of the new borrower, the fee may be the greater of $400 or 1 percent of the unpaid principal balance up to $900, plus out-of-pocket costs. Where no credit approval is required, the minimum fee is $100. The lender can charge lower fees if his costs warrant.

If you have obtained satisfactory financing, you are ready to go back to the seller and arrange for a closing date.

ALERT

Be sure to ask for a monthly principal and interest accounting of your loan payments to the lending institution. Also be sure that your payments toward mortgage insurance are to be discontinued when your equity approaches 25–30 percent by virtue of "pay-down" or "appreciation." At this point the lender's risk is eliminated and the insurance coverage is not needed.

NOTE

If you have not been able to obtain suitable financing, you can get out of the contract because of your financing contingency clause, or you and the seller can agree to other suitable terms and proceed with the closing.

NOTES

_____

_____

_____

_____

_____

_____

_____

_____

_____

_____

_____

_____

_____

_____

_____

_____

_____

_____

_____

_____

_____

10
CONDOMINIUM TERMS AND PHRASES

It is suggested that you become familiar with these terms and phrases that are found in real estate documents and referred to by realtors and lawyers:

GENERAL DOCUMENTS

Assessment
Proportionate share of the budgeted annual cost to maintain the common areas and to maintain sufficient reserves to assure financial stability. This annual assessment is reduced to monthly charges payable to the association of owners.

Certificate of Title
This is the paper (instrument) that signifies ownership of a unit. It usually contains a legal description of the unit and its relationship to the condominium project as a whole.

Common Area or Common Estate
Generally this encompasses all of a condominium which is not specifically delineated and described as a dwelling unit, e.g., drives, parking areas, recreational areas, etc.

Common or Undivided Interest
Joint ownership with other fee owners of all land and areas within the structures that are not described as individually owned units.

Condominium Association, Association of Owners, Condominium Association Board of Directors, or Council of Co-Owners
The governing body of a condominium elected by and selected from the unit owners. Its authority to operate comes from the declaration.

Condominium Regime
The mode of self-rule established when condominium documents are recorded. This term also refers to all the documents necessary to legally constitute a condominium to operate as such.

Delineate
To describe the physical boundaries of a dwelling unit in a condominium.

Latent Defect Bond
An assurance required by HUD-FHA that defects due to faulty materials and workmanship, which are found within a year of the date of completion, will be corrected by the builder (similar to Builder's Warranty).

Liability and Hazard Insurance
Insurance to protect against negligent actions of the association of owners and damages caused by fire, wind storm, and other common hazards.

Mortgage Commitment
The written notice from the bank or other lender saying that it will advance the mortgage funds in a specified amount and rate to enable purchase of a unit.

Plot and Plans
Drawings used by surveyors and architects to show the exact location of utilities, streets, common areas, buildings, and units within the buildings in relation to the boundary lines of the total property.

Repair and Maintenance
The costs incurred in replacing damaged items or maintaining housing systems to prevent damage. Usually the association maintains the common areas and the individual unit owner maintains the interior of his unit. Responsibility for maintenance of roof and exterior responsibility differs in developments.

Reserve Funds (Replacement Funds)
Funds which are accumulated on a monthly basis to provide for possible contingencies.

Undivided Interest
In condominium law, the joint ownership of common areas in which the individual percentages are known, but which are not applied to separate the areas physically.

Unit Value Ratio
A percentage figured out by dividing the appraised value of a unit by the total value of all units, thus determining the percentage of votes the owner of the unit has in the government of the common estate and the percentage of operating costs of the common area the unit owner must bear.

CONDOMINIUM DOCUMENTS

Bylaws
Establishes a plan for governing the condominium and generally encompasses the following: owner responsibilities, board officers/directors responsibilities, the rights and responsibilities of the owners as individuals and the individuals as co-owners, e.g., use and maintenance of common areas, establishment of an operating budget, collection of monthly charges/assessments, rules for recreational areas, etc.

Declaration
A document which contains conditions, covenants, and restrictions governing the sale, ownership, use, and disposition of a condominium unit within the framework of applicable state condominium laws.

Management Agreement
The method and form of administration is normally outlined in the declaration. Usually accomplished by the grantor (seller) until the first annual meeting at which time an association board will be elected by and selected from among the owners.

Operating Budget
Scheduling of estimates or existing monthly costs and contingency reserves necessary for maintenance of grounds, building exteriors, interiors, recreational areas, common areas, etc.

Pre-Sale Agreement
Lending institutions usually will, and should, require that at least 50 percent of the condominium units in a new or conversion development be sold before they will allow any of the buyers to close. (NOTE: In most cases, the developer will allow the approved buyer to move in and pay rent until the 50 percent requirement has been met.)

Regulatory Agreement
Used in the HUD-FHA regulated condominiums. The regulatory agreement is an agreement between the condominium association of owners and HUD-FHA for the purpose of establishing eligibility for mortgage insurance. It is intended to ensure that a condominium project conforms to certain requirements under Section 234 of the National Housing Act (including consumer protection). It also protects HUD-FHA's insured interest.

Subscription Purchase Agreement
Basically a sales or purchase contract (refer to Purchase Contract checklist). It should disclose all pertinent facts concerning the condominium, detail the buyer's interest attached to his unit, make known the existence of other condominium documents, and include language of a properly drafted sales contract as required by the state.

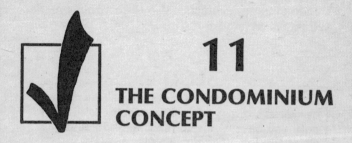

11
THE CONDOMINIUM CONCEPT

Condominiums come in many forms, from inner-city structures to suburban town houses. Some are designed and built as new, while others are conversions of older rental units. There are specific differences in this type of ownership and you should be sure that you understand the concept.

Remain Alert and Note the Following Condominium Facts:

• Condominiums are not covered under federal law. (There is, however, a law covering mortgages issued by HUD-FHA.)

- Condominiums are covered under specific laws in the state where they are located. (NOTE: Laws differ from state to state.)
- Condominium documents also differ from one development to another.

ALERT

Don't sign a subscription and/or purchase agreement, or any other form of sales contract, until you have received, read, and fully understood the following documents.

ALERT	OK	
☐	☐	**DECLARATION**
☐	☐	**BYLAWS**
☐	☐	**OPERATING BUDGET**
☐	☐	**MANAGEMENT AGREEMENT**
☐	☐	**SALES CONTRACT AND/OR SUBSCRIPTION AGREEMENT**
☐	☐	**REGULATORY AGREEMENT (if any mortgage in the project is HUD-FHA insured)**

ALERT

Make sure that you understand these documents! Refer to Condominium Terms, Phrases, and Documents, pages 79-83.

ALERT OK

☐ ☐ **OTHER OBSERVATIONS:** If you find something in addition to the points above that ''alerts'' you, check this ALERT box and list the item under ''Notes'' on page 94.

Obtain a satisfactory answer for any ALERT box that you have checked!

ALERT OK

☐ ☐ **DOWN PAYMENT:** Don't make a down payment until you are positive you will receive your mortgage loan or that the purchase agreement states that your down payment will be refunded if you are unable to get the financing you want and need.

☐ ☐ **ASK ABOUT CLOSING COSTS:** Cash over and above your down payment? How much?

☐ ☐ **UNDERSTANDING THE OPERATING BUDGET:** Can you afford the monthly assessments and their probable inflation—indexed, yearly increases? Determine your approximate total monthly expenses, e.g., mortgage payments, insurance, taxes, assessments, utilities, and other living expenses. You will have to live with this total, as well as inflationary increases. Be safe now, not sorry later.

ALERT   OK

☐   ☐   **MASTER HAZARD AND LIABIL-ITY INSURANCE POLICIES:** The hazard policy (fire and other perils) should have a property endorsement recognizing all the unit owners as beneficiaries. The liability policy should have sufficient liability coverage naming as insured the entire development, the board of directors, and each unit owner individually as co-owners. Ask for specimen copies. Check them. Understand them.

☐   ☐   **SUFFICIENT CAPITAL:** Does the developer have sufficient capital to complete the entire project without using your down payment for working capital?

NOTE _____

Some states require that down payments be deposited into an escrow account. Ask about it!

ALERT   OK

☐   ☐   **FUTURE DEVELOPMENT:** Is what you see the entire development, or does the developer plan to enlarge the project by adding more land and units? This could effect your percentage of interest at the time of purchase. Further development could drastically change the view, e.g., waterfront, woods, etc., from your unit.

ALERT   OK

☐   ☐   **DEFAULT PROTECTION:** Determine if there is a liquidated damage clause (Buyer Default Clause) in the sales/purchase agreement. You do not want to be responsible for anything but your down payment in the event that you would default (*see* Purchase Contract checklist).

☐   ☐   **RIGHT-TO-SELL RESTRICTIONS:** Do you have the right to sell your unit on the open market or must you first offer it to the association for a stipulated period of time? This would contradict "fee simply ownership" which carries the undisputed right of disposal. (NOTE: Remember that HUD-FHA will not allow this restriction.)

☐   ☐   **HAVE ALL STATE REQUIREMENTS BEEN MET:** Have all local municipal building codes been met? Check with your state Real Estate Commission, local Real Estate Board and Building Department.

☐   ☐   **ANY HIDDEN LEASEHOLD COSTS:** Some developers retain ownership of part of the project, usually the recreational facilities and sometimes the land, and then lease them back to the owners for 99 years. Be aware of the differences between full ownership (fee simple title) control and leasehold (giving developers control).

ALERT   OK

☐   ☐   **DEVELOPER CONTROL:** If a developer should purchase or retain ownership of one or more units, he could prevent any change in the declaration not to his liking. (NOTE: Changes in the declaration normally require the consent of all of the owners, not just the developer.)

☐   ☐   **OTHER OBSERVATIONS:** If you find something in addition to the points above that "alerts" you, check this ALERT box and list the item under "Notes" on page 94.

Obtain a satisfactory answer for any ALERT box that you have checked!

ALERT   OK

☐   ☐   **OUTSIDE PROFESSIONAL MANAGEMENT:** Does the declaration give policy-making powers to a professional management company? This action would preempt the powers of the elected board of directors. Neither the board nor the owners would be able to change undesirable situations.

☐   ☐   **BYLAWS:** These are basically the rules and regulations under which the owners live. Are the existing rules reasonable? (NOTE: These rules can be changed at any time by a majority vote of the owners. In a new project, the rules and regula-

ALERT OK

tions in the bylaws are determined at the first annual meeting.)

☐ ☐ **ACKNOWLEDGMENT COVENANT:** Do the declaration or bylaws contain a covenant that the purchase, rental, or occupancy of a unit signifies the acceptance of and compliance with the bylaws? Such a clause stipulates that every occupant must abide by the rules and regulations.

☐ ☐ **PRIVACY AND CONVENIENCE:** What are the views from your windows? Into your windows? How close are the patios, decks, or porches? Are the walls soundproof? Is there enough parking for guests? Where do you park? (*see* Home Inspection checklist—Livability Features.)

☐ ☐ **CONTINGENCY RESERVE FUND:** Has this been provided for in the declaration or bylaws? It is better to set aside small monthly sums to cover long-range replacements or repairs, instead of being unexpectedly charged with a large assessment.

☐ ☐ **RENTERS:** Do the declaration or bylaws control the number of units that may be occupied by renters? Generally speaking, renters do not take the same pride in maintaining property as do owners.

ALERT   OK

☐   ☐   **PRE-SALE AGREEMENT:** This should be included in the purchase contract or subscription when buying a condominium in a new or conversion development (*see* Condominium Terms and Phrases).

☐   ☐   **OTHER OBSERVATIONS:** If you find something in addition to the points above that "alerts" you, check this ALERT box and list the item under "Notes" below.

Obtain a satisfactory answer for any ALERT box that you have checked!

RESPONSIBILITIES

- The owner must be capable of bearing his/her own mortgage payments, current/future expenses, assessments, and taxes; therefore, an owner's title is not endangered by default on the part of other owners.
- The owner must be capable of bearing current expenses, assessments, taxes, and any future inflationary increases.
- The owner must abide by all rules and regulations set forth in the declaration or bylaws. There is some flexibility in the bylaws because rules and regulations can be changed by a majority vote of the owners; however, be alert to the fact that it takes the vote of

all of the owners to change any rule or regulation found in the declaration.

- The owner should assume an active role in the association management by running for office on the board of directors or participating in the meetings and voting on the issues which affect day-to-day living conditions.

TAX CHARACTERISTICS

All taxes must be levied against the individual unit separately and not against the whole condominium development. Tax advantages are the same as for a conventional homeowner in that you may deduct real estate taxes and mortgage interest from income for federal tax purposes.

NOTES

Before you proceed with this purchase, obtain satisfactory answers for any item you have listed below and for any ALERT boxes checked.

12
THE COOPERATIVE CONCEPT

The cooperative, the forerunner of condominiums, is still available in some areas such as New York and Chicago. The buyer does not actually own the real estate; instead, the buyer receives a share in the corporation that owns the building, and is given a proprietary lease to the unit/apartment.

ALERT   OK

☐   ☐   Be sure to have a financing contingency in your purchase contract. Financing is difficult because there is not individual ownership in each unit.

☐   ☐   Check to see what amount of liability you will be assuming for your share of the existing mortgage on the building. This would be in addition to any loan you might obtain to buy your share.

95

NOTE _____

For tax purposes, you may deduct your share of the taxes levied against the building. The IRS will allow the interest on your loan to be treated as a mortgage and allow a deduction.

Use this checklist along with the preceding Home Inspection, Community and Neighborhood, Purchase Contract, and Contingency Home Inspection checklists.

APPENDIX 1
HOMEOWNERS INSURANCE

Now That You Have Purchased Your Home, Protect Your Investment.

The best advice is to consult a properly licensed professional insurance agent. Listen carefully to the advice given; however, do not hesitate to question anything that you do not understand.

Here Are the Key Areas of Coverage That You Should Consider:

ALERT OK

☐   ☐ **PROPER INSURANCE TO VALUE**

☐   ☐ **RECOVERY BASIS AT THE TIME OF LOSS**

☐   ☐ **LIMITED COVERAGE ON SOME PROPERTY**

ALERT   OK

☐   ☐   **EXCLUDED PROPERTY**

☐   ☐   **PERILS INCLUDED**

☐   ☐   **DEDUCTIBLES**

☐   ☐   **LIABILITY COVERAGE**

For instance, it is recommended that you insure your home for 100 percent of the replacement cost of the dwelling and make certain that the amount of insurance keeps pace with increases in local construction costs. On a new home the replacement cost can be easily obtained from the builder. On an older home, builders in the area familiar with the type of construction may be able to calculate a replacement cost. In addition, most insurance agents have access to replacement cost estimators. Discuss this and the other items above with your insurance agent.

APPENDIX 2
TAX INFORMATION

NOTE

Due to complex changing tax laws and their many different applications, the following information is not complete or in-depth. Seek advice from your accountant, tax lawyer and/or your local Internal Revenue Service office. Excellent IRS publications are available at little or no cost. A list of suggested publications has been included at the end of this section for your convenience.

ALERT

There are excellent tax advantages and deductions available and allowable. Take full advantage of them. Keep full records of all transactions and expenses involved in buying, owning, and selling your home. Keep all records for at least three (3) years after you have sold your home. Here are a few tips.

WHEN YOU ARE BUYING

Keep full and accurate records of your purchase price (down payment plus mortgage) and all other costs of purchase, such as real estate fees, legal fees, transfer taxes, etc. All of these amount to your original cost basis.

OWNING YOUR HOME

An adjusted basis is your original cost basis, increased or decreased by certain amounts. You increase the cost basis by the costs of improvements that materially add to the value of your home, considerably prolong its useful life, or adapt it to new uses. Finishing a basement room, putting up a fence, installing a new roof, or paving your driveway are examples of costs that are added to your basis. "Repairs" keep your home in a good, efficient operating condition. Interior and exterior painting, fixing your gutters or floors, mending leaks or replacing broken windows are examples of repairs. Repairs do not add to the basis of your home and are not deductible unless your home is used for business.

_____ ALERT _____

You should distinguish carefully between repairs and improvements, and keep accurate records. Your original cost basis is reduced by items such as energy credits allowed, depreciation taken, etc.

SELLING YOUR HOME

Amount Realized on the Sale. This is the selling price reduced by any expenses of the sale; for example, real estate commission, title insurance, legal fees, transfer taxes, etc.

Adjusted Sales Price. This is the amount realized on the sale reduced by qualified fixing-up expenses; for example, painting, redecorating, new shrubs, etc. Fixing up expenses must be paid for within 30 days after the residence is sold. The work (fixing-up) must have been done during the 90 days before the day the sales contract was signed.

Capital Gain Exemptions. If you, the seller (taxpayer), buy or build a new home within a period of two years before or two years after the sale of your home, any gain is recognized only if the adjusted sales price of the old home exceeds that of the new home. (NOTE: Both the old and new homes must be places of your principal residence.)

Example: You originally purchased your home in 1975 for the sum of $50,000. You sold this home in January 1990 for the sum of $90,000. You purchased another home in April 1990 for the sum of $105,000. The $40,000 gain is not IRS recognizable. However, if your new home costs only $80,000, then you would have a recognized gain of $10,000—realized gain/profit not reinvested in a new home.

Once-in-a-Lifetime Capital Gain Exclusion. Taxpayers aged 55 or older prior to the date of the sale of a principal residence may elect to exclude up to $125,000 of the gain realized on this sale. Example:

Sale price	$ 200,000
Adjusted basis of home	50,000
Gain realized	150,000
Less exclusion	125,000
Gain recognized	$ 25,000

NOTE

As mentioned previously, there are many tax advantages, deductions, and applications. It is recommended that you take full advantage of the services offered by the Internal Revenue Service (IRS). Their consultants stand ready to assist you at any time and they offer many excellent publications for use.

The following is a partial list of IRS publications applicable to home buying, owning, and selling, and information as to how you may obtain them.

PUBLICATION

523	Tax Information on Selling Your Home
2119	Sale or Exchange of Principal Residence
903	Energy Credits for Individuals
5695	Residential Energy Credit

529	Miscellaneous Deductions
530	Tax Information for Homeowners
545	Interest Expense
551	Basis of Assets
588	Condominiums, Cooperative Apartments and Homeowners Associations

HOW TO GET IRS FORMS AND PUBLICATIONS

You can order tax forms and publications from the IRS Forms Distribution Center for your state at the address below. Or, if you prefer, you can photocopy tax forms from reproducible copies kept at many public libraries. In addition, many libraries have reference sets of IRS publications which you can read or copy on the spot.

IF YOU ARE LOCATED IN: SEND TO:

"Forms Distribution Center" (for your state)

Alaska, Arizona, California, Hawaii, Idaho, Montana, Nevada, Oregon, Utah, Washington

P. O. Box 11906
Fresno, CA 93775

Arkansas, Colorado, Kansas, Louisiana, New Mexico, Oklahoma, Texas, Wyoming

P. O. Box 2923
Austin, TX 78769

Illinois, Iowa, Minnesota, Missouri, Nebraska, North Dakota, South Dakota, Wisconsin	P. O. Box 1040 Kansas City, MO 64141
Indiana, Kentucky, Michigan, Ohio, West Virginia	P. O. Box 145500 Cincinnati, OH 45214
Alabama, Florida, Georgia, Mississippi, North Carolina, South Carolina, Tennessee	Caller No. 1010 Atlanta, GA 30370
Connecticut, Maine, Massachusetts, New Hampshire, Eastern New York (including New York City), Rhode Island, Vermont	P. O. Box 2333 Methuen, MA 01844
Western New York	P. O. Box 260 Buffalo, NY 14201
Delaware, District of Columbia, Maryland, New Jersey, Pennsylvania, Virginia	P. O. Box 27322 Richmond, VA 23261

FOREIGN ADDRESSES AND EXCEPTIONS

FOREIGN ADDRESSES: Taxpayers with mailing addresses in foreign countries should send their requests for forms and publications to:

> IRS Distribution Center
> P. O. Box 25866
> Richmond, VA 23260

PUERTO RICO:

> Director's Representative
> U.S. Internal Revenue Service
> Federal Office Building
> Chardon Street
> Hato Rey, PR 00918

VIRGIN ISLANDS:

> Departments of Finance
> Tax Division
> Charlotte Amalie
> St. Thomas, VI 00801

GUAM:

> U.S. Internal Revenue Service
> 4th Floor
> Pacific Daily News Building
> P. O. Box 3645
> Agana, GU 96910

APPENDIX 3

PREPARING YOUR HOME FOR SALE

These checklists are designed to help you realize a faster and more profitable sale. Buyers will notice and might react negatively to clutter, dirt, odors, lack of maintenance, and cramped rooms and storage areas. Follow these checklists and check each item when you are sure it is acceptable to the buyer.

NOTE

Some of the following check items will not be applicable to condominium owners.

ALERT OK

☐   ☐   **CLUTTER REMOVAL AND STOR-AGE:** Clear out your closets, cupboards, attic, and garage. Have a garage sale or give away all accumulated, not really needed items. Clean or paint the storage areas and neatly store the remaining

ALERT   OK

items. Store any excess items in one of
the convenient mini-storage warehouses
until you have sold. (NOTE: Your closets
and storage areas will now appear larger
to the potential buyer.)

☐   ☐   **FLOORS:** Polish, repair, or replace
tiles and linoleum. Clean or replace carpeting as needed. Apply new stair treads
if needed. Scrub and hose down the basement floor.

☐   ☐   **WALLS:** Paint or repaper where needed. It is not necessary to change your
decorating scheme; you just want to present a clean, fresh look. Dark or stained
basement walls should be washed down
or repainted.

☐   ☐   **DRAPES / CURTAINS / BLINDS:**
There should be in good repair. Clean or
replace as needed.

☐   ☐   **SWITCHES / LIGHTING FIX-
TURES, ETC.:** Replace burned out
bulbs. Clean or replace shades, lenses,
covers, etc. Check all switches for
operation.

☐   ☐   **WINDOWS / STORM WINDOWS /
SCREENS:** These should be clean and
in good repair. Make sure that they all
work freely; unopenable windows are a
firetrap and cost a lot to replace.

ALERT OK

☐ ☐ **DOORS/STORM DOORS/SCREENS:** Clean, repaint or restain as needed. Replace, repair, or polish/clean hardware. All doors should open and close easily and freely. Oil any hinges that squeak.

☐ ☐ **PLUMBING:** Repair dripping faucets, running or noisy toilets, and clogged or slow drains. Clean, re-enamel, or replace badly stained or chipped sinks, tubs, and toilet bowls.

☐ ☐ **APPLIANCES:** Clean and polish all appliances—stove, refrigerator, washer, dryer, etc. Special attention should be given to stove top burners and the ventilating hood and fan.

☐ ☐ **FURNITURE:** Accumulated furniture is comfortable and homey; however, too much could give the impression of small rooms. Store excess furniture until after the sale.

☐ ☐ **EXTERIOR:** Clean, paint, repair, or replace shutters, siding, all wood trim, roof shingles, gutters, downspouts, lamp posts, mailboxes, fencing, air conditioners, or heat pumps. Check caulking around doors and windows, and replace if necessary.

☐ ☐ **GARAGE:** Remove oil stains from floor. Paint or clean walls, shelving, or

ALERT   OK

storage cabinets. Neatly store needed items. Storing excess items until after the sale will give the garage a larger appearance.

□   □   **SIDEWALKS/STEPS/DRIVEWAY:** Repair or replace broken sections. Resurface or retop driveway if needed.

□   □   **PORCHES / PATIOS / DECKS:** Clean, resurface, paint, or stain as needed.

□   □   **LAWN:** Resod or reseed weak areas as needed. Keep neatly cut, and water for greenness.

□   □   **TREES AND SHRUBS:** Cut out all dead or dying branches. Remove any dead trees, flowers, or shrubs. Trim back all shrubs. If shrubs have overgrown and will not trim back neatly, it is then suggested that you replace these with new plants. Trim and weed all garden space. Mulch where applicable (around trees, shrubs, flower beds, etc).

□   □   **OUTSIDE STORAGE:** Trailers, boats, campers, additional automobiles, etc. should be stored elsewhere until after the sale. Any items that must be stored in the outside area should be neatly stored and/or covered.

HOUSECLEANING TIPS

- Use newspapers along with glass cleaners to clean and polish windows and mirrors. Use a lemon-scented cleaner for cabinets and painted surfaces. Use a small amount of ammonia along with cleanser in water for floors, inside of cabinets, under the sink, etc.
- Replace old mildewed shower curtains and bath mats.
- Clean dirt and grime out of all cornices, crevices, etc. Clean and scrub—polish and rub!

Hints, Tips, and Reminders for Your Open House

- House should be clean and neat. Beds should be made, dishes washed, sink clean, garbage out, towels fresh, soiled laundry in laundry room containers.
- Have fresh flowers about, something baking in the oven, fire in the fireplace in season, soft music in the background, etc. The entire home should be light and cheerful.
- Have available the last twelve months' utility bills, and all instruction manuals and warranties for appliances, furnaces, etc.
- Have available a list of all items that you intend to exclude from the sale—specific light fixtures, large mirrors, fireplace equipment, draperies, carpeting, etc.
- Keep small valuables out of sight—don't invite an incident.

- Allow your salesperson to answer the questions of the buyer. If questions are directed to you, answer fully and honestly.

These checklists were designed to help you prepare your house for sale; however, you may find that additional items need your attention.

NOTES

Before you show your house, take care of any ALERT boxes checked.

_____

_____

_____

_____

_____

_____

_____

_____

_____

_____

_____

_____

_____

_____

_____

_____

_____

_____

_____

_____

INDEX